To Dear Mary,

In memory of your time in Australia

Love from Lawrie, Joan & a dear lady
from our Church who has enjoyed
your shows, but wishes to be nameless

OUTBACK
REFLECTIONS

OUTBACK
REFLECTIONS

AUB PODLICH
BRUCE PREWER

with photographs by
JOCELYN BURT
CHRIS SPIKER
Additional photography by Aub Podlich

Photographs not credited in the captions are by Jocelyn Burt

LEFT: *Spring wildflowers, Chambers Pillar, NT*

 **Lutheran Publishing House**

Graphic design by Graeme Cogdell

First printing August 1991

National Library of Australia Cataloguing-in-Publication entry

Podlich, Aubrey, 1946–
  Outback reflections.

  ISBN 0 85910 569 5.

  1. Christian poetry, Australian. 2. Australia — Description and travel. I. Prewer, Bruce D.
  (Bruce David), 1931–   . II. Burt, Jocelyn. III. Spiker, Chris. IV. Title.

A821.3080382

Colour separations by Image Colour
Printed by Finsbury Press

Published by Lutheran Publishing House,
205 Halifax Street, Adelaide, South Australia LPH 91-0511

INTRODUCTION

He had few qualifications and little experience. To the establishment, his announced intention of finding an overland route from Queensland's Darling Downs to Port Essington in the Northern Territory, a distance of nearly 5000 kilometres, was nothing short of an impertinence. He wasn't even an Englishman! Major Thomas Mitchell, the establishment's official explorer, labelled the insatiably curious, fiercely determined Prussian Ludwig Leichhardt 'a damned foreign coaster!' Fifteen months after leaving Jimbour station, and long given up for dead, the Leichhardt party, having beaten all the incredible rigours of the bush and survived Aboriginal attack, stumbled into Port Essington. Leichhardt, returning to Sydney in time to hear his own funeral dirge being sung, became a colony's hero.

However, on his third expedition, in 1848, there was to be no resurrection. Leichhardt set out again on a most ambitious attempt to cross Australia from the very margins of white settlement at Mount Abundance near Roma in Queensland, to present-day Perth in Western Australia. The land opened its mouth and swallowed him, his six companions, their eight horses, 50 bullocks, 20 mules, and all their provisions. No trace of that entire party has ever been found, its ultimate fate remaining one of the most closely guarded secrets of the Australian outback.

LEFT: *Curdimurka railway siding, Oodnadatta Track, SA*
UPPER RIGHT: *Distant view of the Olgas, Uluru National Park, NT*
LOWER RIGHT: *N'Dhala Gorge, NT*

UPPER LEFT: *Kangaroo jawbone* PODLICH
LOWER LEFT: *Sand-dunes, Eucla, WA*
UPPER RIGHT: *Old wagon, and ruins of the Warrina railway siding, Oodnadatta Track, SA*
LOWER RIGHT: *The Channel Country in drought, near Birdsville, Qld*

Leichhardt and his men were not the first curious and determined 'damned foreign coasters' to be swallowed by the Australian outback, nor would they be the last. Australia's arid interior has drawn people to itself for untold thousands of generations. Many whom the land clasped to herself never returned, an ominous reminder that this vast area of God's harsher Eden was never to be underestimated or taken for granted. The outback, as a recent tragic news story about the deaths of four stranded Aboriginal travellers grimly illustrates, can be relentlessly unforgiving. Yet for all that — perhaps partly because of it — the Australian outback has a lure and a fascination for Australians which touches familiar chords in the mind of this nation of coast-huggers and city-dwellers. Looming large among all the myths which describe us as a people is the outback, dreaded, mysterious, and fascinating.

At the heart of that myth is a lively song about a sheep thief who committed suicide by drowning in an outback waterhole:
> Once a jolly swagman camped
> by a billabong,
> Under the shade of a coolibah
> tree.

Never mind that most Australians wouldn't know a coolibah if they did camp under it, couldn't distinguish a billabong from a bilby, and will never see a genuine swagman — 'Waltzing Matilda' from Combo Waterhole has become *our* song!

Despite its importance in our national psyche, Australians have difficulty defining the boundaries of the outback. Some suggest that it begins and ends in our own minds! The very term 'outback' for the vast inland of Australia indicates that for most Australians there is a huge part of this land where they not only do not live and work, but where they could never feel at home. Words like 'remote', 'harsh', 'hostile', when applied to the outback, place that area in contrast to life in the settled, civilised, urbanised environments of the seaboards. Australia has few outback cities. We are indeed a whole nation of 'damned foreign coasters', to whom much of our own land will always remain that strange area 'out back' from our day-to-day existence.

For most Australians then, the outback is no more than a tourist destination. More accurately, it is a seemingly endless plain of low unattractive scrub, bulldust, heat, flies, stones, and sometimes rough roads, which must be endured in long tiring days of driving en route to the marvellous places that make all the driving worthwhile, at least once in a lifetime: Uluru, the Olgas, the Flinders Ranges, Kings Canyon, Katherine Gorge, the Kimberleys, the Stockman's Hall of Fame . . .

There can be no denying, even by the most comfort-conscious city visitor, that the natural wonders of the well-known tourist route are magnificent. Bathed in early morning or late afternoon light, the rich colours of the inland are beyond compare, the cliffs and sandhills, folded ranges and snaking

gorges burning with red, purple, yellow, and ochre flames. Landforms and rock sculptures surprise and delight, from the looming sleeping-animal shapes of Uluru and Katatjuta, to the giant beehives of the Bungle Bungles, the smooth sweeping walls of roseate

UPPER LEFT: *Mungo National Park, NSW*
LOWER LEFT: *Ayers Rock, Uluru National Park, NT*

sandstone at Kings Canyon, the
exquisitely rounded, delicately
balanced Devil's Marbles, and the
giant saucer of the Wolf Creek
meteorite crater. Scientific oddities
and visual delights go hand in hand:
remnant rare Livistonia palms in
Palm Valley, dinosaur prints at
Winton, the lime-rich emerald green
water of Lawn Hill Gorge, the
legendary min min lights of
Queensland's west, and the
profusion of desert wildflowers
after rain. Over all this brooding,
eroding, and crumbling landscape
hangs the impression of great age,
and of a wonderful ancient beauty
sculpted and painted by time and
hardship. And who will ever forget
the blaze of outback stars on a clear
inland night?

UPPER RIGHT: *Jabiru Dreaming, Kakadu National
Park, NT*
LOWER RIGHT: *Mulla mullas in bloom, Pilbara, WA*

For those prepared to observe and understand, there are many surprises arising directly from the struggle to live and thrive in an environment where the norm is extremes of both temperature and rainfall. The tough desert acacias — mulga, gidgee, boree, myall, and the expressively named 'dead-finish' — with their fine grey foliage and pleasant form, swarm over vast areas. In other places, graceful casuarinas called desert oaks, clothed in weeping emu-feather plumes, cast welcome shade in an ocean of golden-crowned, sand-stabilising spinifex. Few trees are as starkly beautiful as the gnarled ghost gums which cling to the red cliffs and top-rock country. Along nature's highways, the mostly dry watercourses where phantom rivers run deep underground, thousands of cockatoos, parrots, and honeyeaters ransack the twisting avenues of river red gums and coolibahs for nectar and nesting hollows. The unusual and often showy flowers of grevillea, hakea, emu bush and desert rose grace areas of red sand and rocky outcrops, while few wildflower displays could out-miracle the miracle of previously bare desert plains in bloom after convenient rain. Around Uluru and in all the deep slashes of gorges, the snaking latticework of the roots of Ilyi, the rock fig, is often the first clue to the presence of a harvest of yellow and brown fruit.

Even the most unobservant tourist cannot fail to notice, from the comfort of a moving vehicle, the commonest outback wildlife: red kangaroo and emu, wallaroo in rocky areas, plains turkey and wedge-tailed eagle, little flocks of finches, galahs, and budgies, and

UPPER LEFT: Emu SPIKER
LOWER LEFT: Finke River and Mount Sonder, NT

even an occasional curious dingo. But for the dedicated and persistent, there are even greater rewards: the remarkable shield shrimps in ephemeral rock pools on top of Uluru, the blind marsupial mole which 'swims' along underground in the sandhills, the etchings of a thousand footprints on the sands, of nocturnal creatures such as hopping mice, bilby, dunnart, gecko, and mulgara. Deep under the ground, safe in their cavities, lie those amazing living reservoirs, the honey-pot ants, and the water-storing frogs.

Evocative as it is of large, classical themes, it is perhaps fitting that the outback should embrace the very heart of Australia. Here the struggle between life and death is always apparent. The vastness of the land reduces human beings to a wholesome humility. In places like this we are recalled to the value of simple things: the priceless nature of water, of shade, of life, and of death, on which all life feeds. Here there is always more to life than meets the eye, always so much going on under the surface. Here the vast flat wilderness draws to our surfaces the simultaneous emotions of ecstasy and terror. The long straight roads remind us that life is a journey through ordinary, but ever more surprising places, via the few spectacular memories dotted along the way. The beautiful, the special, the holy, must be found in the ordinary, if they are to be found at all. And everywhere, and over everything, hovers this sense of something, someone, greater.

UPPER RIGHT: *Red kangaroo* SPIKER
FAR RIGHT: *Thorny devil* SPIKER
LOWER RIGHT: *Wedge-tailed eagle* SPIKER

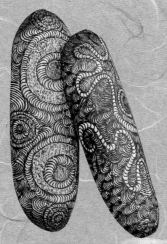

Nor can we ever forget that what for most Australians is remote and somewhere 'out back', is for many others 'home', a home treasured and loved and part of their very lifeblood. White Australians, thinking of people in the outback, recall the history, myths, and exploits of explorers, shearers, drovers, and pastoralists. Our tradition abounds with stories of courageous men and women pioneers who pushed their mobs deeper and deeper along the inland waterholes in search of Australia's most economically valuable plants, the grasses. The modern equivalents of those people still harvest the grass with flocks and herds, mustering their stock with horses and dogs, helicopters and motorbikes.

There are outback towns where people live in incongruous lawned oases of suburbia in the desert, mining camps and missions, outstations and tourist resorts. To

many of these more recent arrivals the outback has become their permanent home, and they in turn have incarnated the Australian spirit of gameness, endurance, and easy-going mateship. This is the land of remarkable people and remarkable achievements: Flynn of the Inland, the Flying Doctor, Qantas, Traeger's pedal wireless, the Overland Telegraph, School of the Air, giant road trains, epic cattle drives, windmills, hot gushing artesian water, and solar-powered telephones. It is also the source of the nation's 'soul', some of our most famous art and literature.

Sometimes omitted in the scripting of the history of the outback are its first inhabitants, the many different Australian Aboriginal peoples. These other outback people possess a wealth of accumulated knowledge and wisdom of living in the outback for untold generations, and this lies often untouched by white society. While we recall the struggles and failures of our early white explorers of the outback: Bourke and Wills, Sturt, Leichhardt, Gosse, Lasseter, and the

hardship suffered by white pioneers 'beyond the never-never', we forget what wonderful skills were possessed by these remarkable and resilient original inhabitants of the land. They lived in all this apparent harshness as we live in suburbia. Theirs were the secrets of the water places, the sources of bush food, the fire-farming of the vegetation, and the different emphases of the turning seasons. They were our first artists, singers, and poets, and our first and finest bushmen, explorers, and pioneers. Their 'song-lines' or 'Dreaming-tracks', the routes invisible to white people, which dwarfed the famous Birdsville and Strzelecki Tracks, or the Canning Stock Route, sang them step by step right across the arid inland, through the territories of neighbours whose languages were as foreign to them as English is to Chinese. Their contribution to the modern pastoral industry remains largely undocumented and unrecognised in the 'official' records of that industry. These people who left no imposing monuments, built no roads, no massive cities, buildings, or military bases, who husbanded a most fragile environment, have much to teach all Australians about the basics and priorities of life on earth. We would do well to listen, and learn.

The outback ultimately does not belong to us. The very nature of the land itself ought to be testimony enough to that. This fragile ecosystem belongs to the Lord, and, as part of that ecosystem, we are honoured with the responsibility of living in it in such a way that the land itself benefits from our presence. This is the challenge to which every Australian is called, whether we are a once-in-a-lifetime visitor — 'a damned foreign coaster' — or whether we are among those fortunate enough to call the Australian outback our home.

March 1991

Aub Podlich

THE COLOUR OF SILENCE

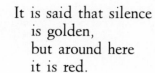

It is said that silence
    is golden,
    but around here
    it is red.

Red as serrated mountains,
    like Dreamtime dinosaurs
    slumbering in the sun.

Red as the warm sand
    among the emu bushes
    and between one's toes.

Red as a desert sunrise
    kissing the ghost gums
    and transfusing the sky.

Red as the blood of the Friend
    who comes with us
    to the end of the world.

PREWER

LEFT: *Cooper Creek in flood, near Etadunna, at sunset, SA*
UPPER RIGHT: *Yampire Gorge, Hamersley Range National Park, WA*
LOWER RIGHT: *Chambers Pillar at sunset*

ULURU

LEFT: *Ayers Rock, Uluru National Park, NT*
RIGHT: *Climbing Ayers Rock*
OVERLEAF: *Devil's Marbles, NT*

Ant people, ant people,
up and down the rock;
ant people, ant people,
climbing by the clock.

Up and down, up and down,
some with ease, some with pain;
the day ends, another dawns,
up and down they stream again.

From air-conditioned buses,
they have not come to stay;
into cars and off to Alice,
hurrying to get away.

White illusion: see and conquer,
mount it and stand tall;
photographs to prove they did it,
but no print upon the soul.

Great icon from the Dreaming
hides its secret worth;
only the pure in heart and meek
shall inherit this earth.

Ant people, ant people,
up and down the rock;
ant people, ant people,
climbing by the clock.

PREWER

GHOST GUM

You call them ghost gums,
but such majesty
will always be
the Holy Ghost's gums
to the likes of me.

PODLICH

UPPER RIGHT: *White gums* (Eucalyptus alba) SPIKER
LOWER RIGHT: *The Twin Ghost Gums, near Alice Springs, NT*

WAITING FOR RAIN

The red dusty land
longs for summer storms
to green the grass
and call emu, euro,
plains turkey, back again.

Life rolls in
on a wild wind.

From earth as dry
and red as this,
the Lord shaped our kin
and greened them
with his own life-giving breath.

So grace us, Lord Jesus,
with your refreshing Spirit;
give us this red earth's resilience
when long suffering
drains our spirits
and dries up our joy
like the face of a parched dam.

We wait with hope
for your cool breath
to green us.

Make us live
and love
again.

PODLICH

LEFT: *A beetle, Simpson Desert*
UPPER RIGHT: *Dried mud, Central Australia*
LOWER RIGHT: *Sand-dune, NT*

DUST

God,
if we're all dust,
and to dust we shall return,
there's sure a lot of us
already gone back
to the great outback!

PODLICH

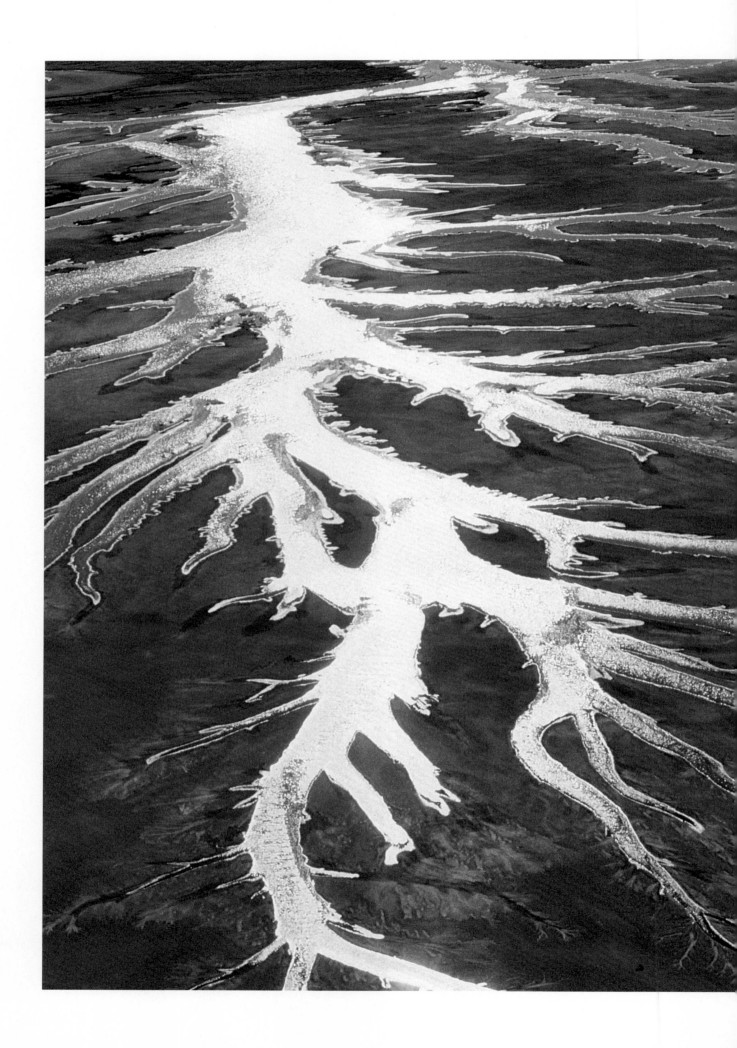

PROGRESS

The land is a Pintubi painting
from the air,
all dots and circles.
The only straight lines
are raw slashes
of roads and fences,
railways and powerlines.

By contrast, nature's highways
are ribbons of trees,
coolibah, ghost gum, red gum,
that snake and twist and curve
around red and brown blotches,
on mosaics of yellow and grey.

Perhaps God's idea
of getting somewhere
is more circular than ours,
leisurely, and less direct,
in tune with the contours
of the land,
and at one with it.

PODLICH

LEFT: *Tidal erosion patterns, from the air, Derby, WA*
UPPER RIGHT: *Aerial view of the Olgas, Uluru
National Park, NT* SPIKER
LOWER RIGHT: *Jasper, Marble Bar, WA*

MORNING AFTER

How awesome is this place!
How strange the aura here!
The very cliff tops blaze
with a flood of pastel fire,
with a Presence unsuspected
when I blithely spread
my sleeping-bag
in last night's dark. *

A moving flush
creeps down to touch
the face of cliffs,
the tips of ghost gums,
the crowns of hillside spinifex,
and the alert ears
of a single wallaroo.
The very air is tinged
with roseate breath.

Who's there?
I mean to say,
but mouth instead
a quiet prayer,
like a child's tiny knock,
at the smallest crack
in a great king's door.

* *Derived from Genesis 28:16,17*

PODLICH

LEFT: *Glen Helen, west of Alice Springs, NT*
RIGHT: *Manning Gorge, Kimberley, WA*

TAKE OFF YOUR SHOES

Like God, this land.
We don't meet the desert;
   it confronts us,
   uncompromising
   in rock and sand.

Arid plains, bare hills,
are not defined by our names;
   they won't submit,
   cannot be shaped
   by human wills.

Fools err herein.
They work to overpower;
    to control,
    to mould and exploit
    this untameable thing.

Bare feet are better;
the humility to learn
    the desert's ways,
    its secret life,
    its hidden water.

The Lord of the prophets is near:
'I am who I am'.
    Moses and Elijah,
    the Baptist, and Jesus
    grew tall here.

PREWER

UPPER LEFT: *Sand-dune, south-west NSW*
LOWER LEFT: *Chichester Range, Pilbara, WA*
RIGHT: *The Olgas, Uluru National Park, NT*
OVERLEAF: *Sunrise, Yellow Water Lagoon, Kakadu National
Park, NT*

DESERT PARADOX

Here in the desert country,
    where shade is rare
    and even spinifex sporadic,
I experience exquisitely
    the absence of God.

Then I begin to know,
    in every dry creek bed
    and across sand ridges,
that paradoxical Presence
    whose loneliness cried aloud
    on a desolate Friday
when the world turned black.

PREWER

BIRDS

Budgies?
Just God's way
for the mulga to change
its suit of conservative grey
to extrovert green!

Galahs?
Now he's filling
the endless blue
with wheeling storm-clouds,
pink and grey!

Corellas?
Look! He's left his white washing
flapping
on that gidgee tree!

PODLICH

UPPER LEFT: *Corellas, near Birdsville*
LOWER LEFT: *Pink cockatoo feeding on paddymelon* SPIKER
RIGHT: *Pink galah* SPIKER

GHOST GUM ON CLIFF FACE

Look at the magnificence
of this struggling tree,
carved by adversity!
How tenaciously
she wraps arthritic knuckles
round the hard dry stone
where she flourishes
so beautifully!

God of suffering,
the mother of endurance;
of endurance;
the mother of character;
of character,
the mother of hope;
of hope,
the mother of beauty:

Grace me, in suffering,
with the artistry
of this faithful tree.

PODLICH

LEFT: *Yampire Gorge, Hamersley Range National Park, WA*
UPPER RIGHT: *Ghost gum (Eucalyptus papuana), Kings Canyon, NT* PODLICH
LOWER RIGHT: *Keep River National Park, NT*

INLAND AT NIGHT

On my back
in the swag
no wind
cool night
stars almost touchable.
Elemental quietness
so quiet I can hear
my own thoughts
and know them
for what they are.
Last vestiges
of urban anxieties
like python skin
peel away.
Thoughts pause
raw contemplation
wells up
wordless
yet full of wisdom
and iridescent
as the sky.
It is good
to have camped
near Bethel.

PREWER

UPPER LEFT: *Camping*
LOWER LEFT: *Stars in a night sky,
outback NSW*
RIGHT: *Moonrise over the Olgas, Uluru
National Park, NT*
OVERLEAF: *The Pinnacles Desert,
Nambung National Park, WA*

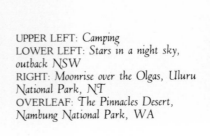

HEAT AND SAND

Fierce country,
strange hard beauty,
most of it not for postcards.
Like its Creator,
not to be taken lightly.

Yet some wise ones,
who seek to live with it
instead of against it,
with the desert creatures
find a homing place
and new prayers.

Sand on a hot wind,
sore eyes and dry tongues,
yet the desert oaks
make parables,
and from deep down
slake their thirst.

It's not for those
who itch to handle and control
even the thing they worship.
The Creator of all this
will be what he will be,
fierce untameable love,
sharing the crosses.

PREWER

UPPER LEFT: *Ayers Rock, Uluru National Park, NT*
LOWER LEFT: *Desert oaks near Kings Canyon, NT*
UPPER RIGHT: *Echidna* SPIKER
LOWER RIGHT: *Man and his camel, Alice Springs, NT*

DRY WATERCOURSE

Don't judge the church
by its surface flow,
when God doesn't seem
to be there;
judge it by the love
its people show.

Under the dry watercourse,
a rich river, far below,
is tapped by flourishing trees.

Searching roots
will always find
the water of life.

The water itself
will draw them.

PODLICH

LEFT: *Glen Helen, west of Alice Springs, NT*
UPPER RIGHT: *Cooper Creek, near the Birdsville Track, SA*
LOWER RIGHT: *Palmer River, NT*

SALVATION

*'He brought me out
into a spacious place;
he rescued me
because he delighted in me.'* *

A single thin-ribbed dingo
picks its way at noon
across an inland sea
of shimmering stones
as wide as the fiery sky.

We saw him
when to our dull eyes
he was only a moving dot.

Hopping mouse and dunnart,
planigale and bilby, you're safe!
In this broad flat expanse
of your Father's hand,
the predator has no place
to lie in wait.

* Psalm 18:19 NIV

PODLICH

UPPER LEFT: *Dunnart* PODLICH
LOWER LEFT: *Sand-dune near Birdsville*
UPPER RIGHT: *Native plague rat* SPIKER
LOWER RIGHT: *Dingo, near Alice Springs*

DALHOUSIE

While the sun sets
     over our shoulders,
the moon rises over the ruins
     of Dalhousie homestead.
Nearby are a few palm trees
     around the springs,
some rusted farm machinery
     and old fencing wire,
and many hectares of paddocks
     filled with nothing but gibbers.

GREY DAYS

Even here in the centre
there are the grey days:
    clouds shroud the sun,
    dead mulga stand stark,
    grey falcons sit huddled,
    a mangy dingo pads by,
    and the gorges are colourless.

Have pity, Lord,
when we mirror such days:
    when feelings stay flat,
    the eye sees no grandeur,
    the heart misses the wonder,
    the spirit crawls low,
    and praise forsakes the lips.

Have pity, Lord,
    and kindle the light
    that comes only
    from within.

UPPER RIGHT: *Near Biloela, Qld*
LOWER RIGHT: *Repeater station, Stuart Highway*

PREWER

MIRAGE

In the mirage
there's a single tree,
and on the tree,
a Man.

Our God is a mirage
without that Man,
'forever receding
as we forever advance', *
without the Man
on the tree
of the cross!

* *Words of Phillip Adams, 1991*

PODLICH

LEFT: *Boab tree at sunrise, east Kimberley, WA*
RIGHT: *Sunrise over riverine forest, Kakadu National Park, NT*
OVERLEAF: *Ayers Rock at sunrise, Uluru National Park, NT*

WILD ASSES

Somewhere south of Finke,
    across the gibber country,
    we travel under afternoon sun,
    hoping this track leads
    to the goal we seek.

No signposts.
    But wild asses turn and watch us,
    their comical heads steady,
    seeming to contain
    an ancient wisdom.

Another wisdom
    gleaned in another land
    in another time and story,
    when stones were ready
    to sing aloud their praises.

We make camp in a gully,
    water scarce, and not sure
    that this is the right track,
    or that our goal is nearer
    than when we started out.

Distant enthusiastic braying
    of donkeys at dusk
    is like sweet gospel,
    telling us the springs we seek
    are nearer than we feared.

Not fools, these creatures
    that survive where we cannot;
    they are to us
    messengers of God
    in a weary land.

PREWER

UPPER LEFT: *Dried mud, outback SA*
LOWER LEFT: *Cattle on outback road, near Maryvale, NT*
UPPER RIGHT: *Wild asses* SPIKER
LOWER RIGHT: *Claypan, near Dalhousie, SA*

STURT'S DESERT PEA

The land's allegories
    meet me everywhere
    and set me singing.
When I look intimately
    into the deep dark eyes
    of the blood-red desert pea,
I imagine I am seeing
    the love-deep eyes
    of my Lord.

PREWER

UPPER LEFT: *Sturt's desert peas*
UPPER RIGHT: *Daisy seed head*
CENTRE RIGHT: *Spring wildflowers, near Wubin, WA*
LOWER RIGHT: *Red sandhill country in spring, south of Alice Springs*

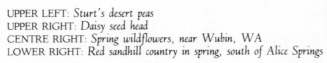

THE GENTLE SEEDS

The seeds of the wilderness
  beyond Ernabella
take no thought for tomorrow.

They neither worry nor fret
  about food or fashion
or disasters which don't happen.

Seeds gently rest
  in the warm womb of the land
and wait for the rains;

the rains that will come,
  this year or next year,
or in twenty years' time.

Then they will awake,
  dance up into life,
and clothe the inland with majesty.

All we who pass by
  with cameras at the ready
may, if we wish, hear them speak:

'O you of little faith,
  rest awhile with us and learn
how dearly loved you are'.

PREWER

STANDLEY CHASM

Soon the sun had moved
forty minutes beyond its zenith,
   having briefly bathed the walls
   with rich aboriginal red.

The midday hubbub is over,
the tourists up and gone,
   the car park is empty,
   the dust settled.

The gorge returns
to the serene solitude
   it has known
   from ancient days.

Some rock wallabies,
which have been in hiding,
   hop out among the stones,
   stretch and sun themselves.

Little plumed pigeons,
colourful and energetic,
   like kindy kids released,
   run down to a pool to drink.

And you, Creator-Spirit,
having observed the noon rush
   and smiled ruefully
   at your human flock,

you watch these contented creatures
of the inland wilderness,
   and you smile sabbatically
   at their pleasure in simple gifts.

PREWER

UPPER LEFT: *Spinifex pigeon* SPIKER
LOWER LEFT: *Crested pigeon, wing detail* PODLICH
RIGHT: *Standley Chasm, MacDonnell Ranges, NT*

OUTBACK PEOPLE

At home in such harshness,
like saltbush and ghost gum,
you've put down your roots
and learnt to belong.

So you inspire us
to love as our home
the dry land around us,
and to reach deeper down,
keeping cool,
staying green.

PODLICH

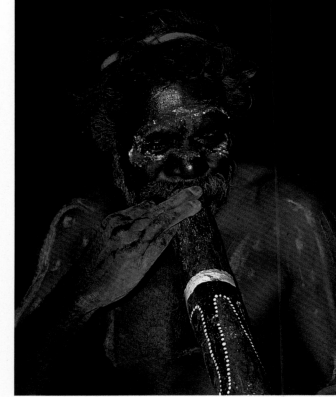

SWEET SANITY

Here,
where the red sand blows,
and distant mountains
elbow themselves up from the plain,
our being chairman of the board,
athlete of the year,
judge of the high court,
or much respected preacher
counts for nothing.

UPPER LEFT: *Aborigine playing a didgeridoo*
LOWER LEFT: *Aboriginal stockman, Birdsville
Track, SA*
BELOW: *MacDonnell Ranges, NT*
OVERLEAF: *Reflections, Finke River at Glen Helen, NT*

We
are the ignorant,
the outsiders
who cannot survive alone
for more than a couple of days,
or understand in a whole lifetime.

Here
the abrasive winds
blow away all pretensions,
and the dunes are ready
to quickly cover human bones.

We
are reduced to size,
and after the first shock,
the affront to our arrogance,
it becomes a healing thing.

Here
we have much to learn;
even the shy animals
can teach us lessons
that stand between life and death.

Here
things go on happening
as they always have, without us,
and in this sweet sanity
we find a new tranquillity.

Here
there is One who comes
from wilderness places, saying:
    'Come unto me, all you
    who labour and are heavy laden,
    and I will give you rest'. *

* *Matthew 11:28*

PREWER

BAOBAB

'*The creation waits in eager expectation.*' *

Fat ladies, weary,
trudging on the plain;
fat ladies with petticoats
bulging with last year's rain,
and hair unkempt.

There's a distant roll of thunder,
and, etched against the flame,
they quicken to the wonder
of the fast-approaching storm.

And in the clouds they glimpse Him
who will claim them brides again,
these fat ladies, tight in skirts,
stepping lightly on the plain.

* *Romans 8:19 NIV*

PODLICH

LEFT: *Boab tree near Fitzroy Crossing, WA*
RIGHT: *Boab tree at sunset, near Derby, WA*

CROCODILE

What could be more tender
than these awful jaws,
jagged with terrible teeth,
gaping carefully,
gently conveying
its little ones
safely from nest to stream?

Who is more tender
than El Shaddai, almighty God,
bursting from such jaws as these
to carry me
to safety?

PODLICH

LEFT: *Saltwater crocodile, Wyndham, WA*
RIGHT: *Freshwater crocodile, Ord River, WA*

DESERT DWELLERS

Lord of the mystic inland,
   I only dare to visit
   the desert places of the spirit
   in the pleasant seasons:
when the rains have been
   and the red sand is carpeted
   with white and gold;
when one can find pleasant pools
   among the rocky places,
   where nymphs become dragonflies;
when the desert animals breed well
   and the dingoes, well fed and sleek,
   find the hunt an easy task;
in such seasons I go exploring
   and cope with minor difficulties,
   pretending I have embraced the truth.

But when the dry times come,
   and the desert shimmers like an oven;
when summer makes travel by day
   a distress and a danger;
when the red sand whirls
   on a fierce savage wind,
   and even shady places
   leave one weary and panting;
then, Lord, I shirk the pain,
   and stay far away in comfort.

Then I leave it to those bold souls
   who trust you in the desert places;
who know and read the summer landscape
   with a love which surpasses sentiment
   and willingly endures the pain.
These who choose to live here,
   not counting the cost,
   have a wisdom and peace
   which is your desert gift.
We, the comfort-holders,
   envy them and laud them,
   but wait for the pleasant seasons,
   and evade the harder learning.

PREWER

UPPER LEFT: *Praying mantis* SPIKER
LOWER LEFT: *Kalamina Gorge, Hamersley Range
National Park, WA*
UPPER RIGHT: *Dingo, Simpson Desert*
LOWER RIGHT: *Hamersley Range, Pilbara, WA*
OVERLEAF: *Windmill, NT*